Say It A Different Way

Say It A Different Way

Poems
Phil Lowe

Edited by
Cathy A. Kodra

One Spirit Press
Portland, Oregon

Printed in the USA

ISBN: 978-1-893075-78-8
ISBN Ebook: 978-1-893075-70-2
LCCN:2011921625

Photography Phil Lowe
Book and Cover Design Spirit Press, LLC

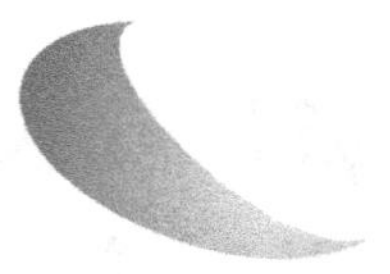

One Spirit Press
www.onespiritpress.com
Portland, Oregon

Dedication

To my wife Betty and daughters Kim and Susan for support over the years while I roamed the country with my camera to capture the beauty of nature and write poems about my experiences.

Publishers Note

One Spirit Press has the philosophy that *words are the breath of life*. The infinite manifestation of life is defined, relished, and explored through words. Phil's work with words draws mind pictures that give form to a unique way of looking through the lens of life. We are proud to present an artist of words and photography.

Acknowledgments

The following poems have been previously published in *Bleeding Hearts: A Sampling of Poems from the Poetry Workshop of the Knoxville Writers' Guild* (Tellico Books, 2009): *Revealed in a Dream: Part I* and *The Rest of the Story: Part II*

Contents

Part I – Free Verse

Part II – Nonets

Part III – Cinquains

Part IV – Letters to the Lord

Introduction

Like strings in the String Theory, words in the mind vibrate according to orientation. People in different parts of the world, and even in different parts of a country, *say it in different ways*, while in the end, it means the same. People in the northeastern part of the U.S. might say, *We hope you come visit again soon,* while in the southern regions the words might be, *Y'all hurry back now.* They ring different bells in the mind, but if the listener hears and understands the words, they serve the same purpose. *Say It a Different Way* strikes notes in diverse minds that might not ring true if struck by the same old stroke.

Words in Motion

As she brushed by me in the doorway
she opined, *It's really cool in there.*

I wasn't sure, should I go back to the car
for a sweater, or was I headed for a rocking
good time? It's hard to tell about words,
what's up can mean *what's going down.*

If words were as clear as the sound of b-flat
and language as universal as a nightingale's
song, editors would be caught in eternal
limbo, interpreters adrift on a silent sea.

When different people with diverse
feelings search for new expressions,
creativity is quick to suggest that we
Say It a Different Way.

Poetry Types Include:

Part I

Free Verse

Free Verse is an irregular form of poetry in which the content is free of traditional rules of versification. (Free from fixed meter or rhyme).

Part II

Nonet

A nonet has nine lines. Line one has 9 syllables, line two, 8 line three, 7 etc. until the end, where line nine finishes with 1 syllable. It can be on any subject and rhyming is optional. Nonets here are presented in true form and in reflection.

Part III

Cinquain

A cinquain is a short, usually unrhymed poem consisting of twenty-two syllables distributed as 2, 4, 6, 8, 2, in five lines. It was developed by the Imagist poet, Adelaide Crapsey. A garland cinquain is a sequence of six cinquains in which the final cinquain is composed of one line from each of the five preceding cinquains.

Part IV

Letters to the Lord

Twenty-one letters in free verse, full of questions not fully answered in Sunday school.

Say It Your Way

When you say it a different way
the world will soon take notice
Morning sun denotes new day
when you say it a different way
Opposing voices have their say
like beetles swarm a lotus
When you say it a different way
the world will soon take notice

Phil Lowe

Knoxville, Tenn.

Part I

Say
It in
Free
Verse

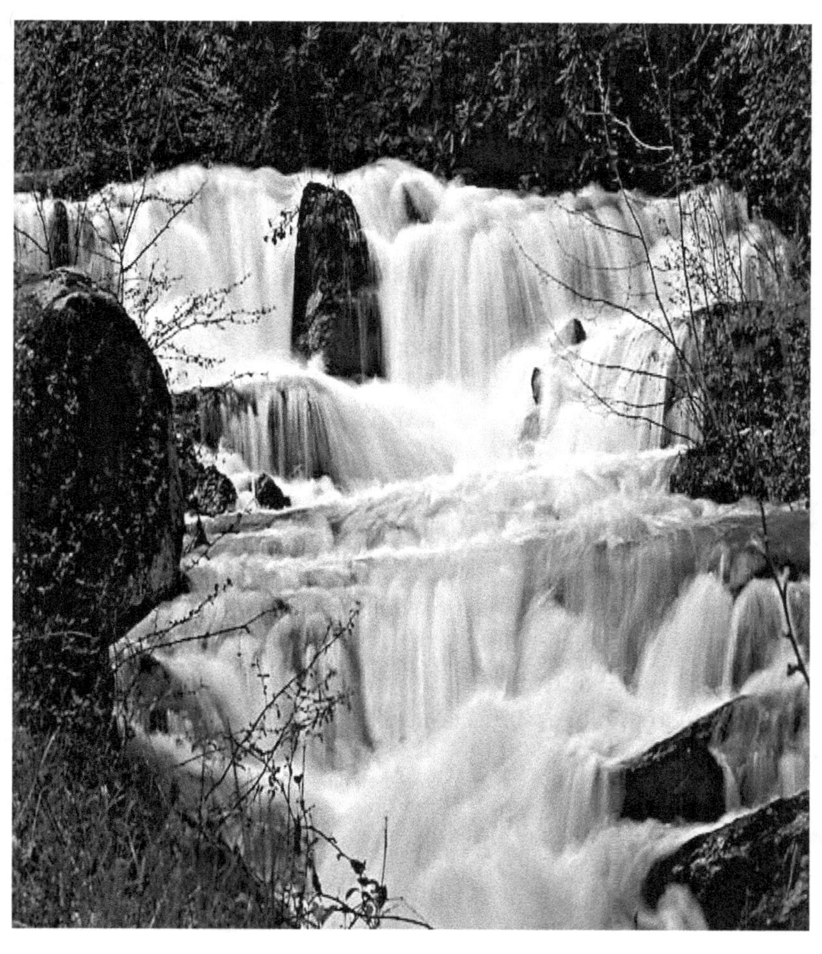

Water cascading
Down a mountain in free fall
Searching for the sea

Puddles and Words

Syntax plummets to paper like raindrops
from misty skies, splatters on fertile soil;
droplets run to settle in crevices
of the mind. By puddles, I fish

for words with compelling sounds
worthy of verse to entice readers
into deeper waters than single words
will lure. I must follow

the muse, sail wind-blown waves,
watch for messages riding whitecaps,
explore new adventure in uncharted
waters near the heartland of soul.

Distant Sounds

Bullfrogs set the rhythm,
ba-rump ba-rump ba-rump.
Cricket's trrrrrrl trrrrrrl
bring melody to song.

From some distant tree
whip-poor-will, whip-poor-will
becomes an obbligato.

Through open doors and windows
only wire screens separate me
from songs of the night, lullabies
of dream land.

Saturday morning movies
brought World War II, newsreels
replaced the music with sounds
of war. Bombs blew away buildings,
rat-a-tat-tat laid waste to human life.

War took a recess, paused
to get its breath, searched
for new lands to rape and plunder,
then, like dogs chasing a rabbit,
leaped after new prey.

Rock and roll twisted, bumped, exploded
into new age expression. Gone from the charts
are *Love is a Many Splendored Thing*
and *A long steel rail and a short crosstie.*

Now war creeps close to home, danger
lurks in planes and trains, music
rocks on, reflecting the times.
From some exquisite place within,

I still hear ba-rump bar-ump ba-rump
and the songs of the night.

Touching Time

Rough wrinkled hands
hold cotton soft new

spanning cycles of time

and what is time?
Life experiences revealed,

winter giving way
to radiant blossoms of spring.

Old and worn
newborn smooth

searching

learning to feel
each other's touch.

Wasp Whispers

It's hard to understand the human
race refusing to live in harmony
with the Creator's plan. No wonder
it is forever engaged in war.

I worked every day in the month
of May building a home for my
children and that man knocked it down
with one swipe of his broom, threw

it into the yard and poured gas, struck
a match and roasted my little ones, all
twelve of them. Cruel, cruel man, I'll
be watching you all summer. I'm not

a vengeful wasp, but that was my family
you so willfully turned into ashes. Next
time I see you sunbathing on your deck,
I'm going to stick my stinger in your butt.

Molded

The critique note said
  Evoke emotion
  make the writing
  more concrete.

I've thought about concrete;
it flows like lumpy gravy,
solidifies, submits
to its mold.

Bombarded by pigeons
and the dog's cocked leg
it gets walked on, spat on,
then cracks, chips, decays.

The strength of concrete is an illusion.

Emotions are like concrete;
they flow through the heart
and harden into ritual,
become dogma in the mind.

How easy for the intellect to think
concrete is absolute.

The Real Me

Rising
floating on air
eyes fixed
on my body below

through the ceiling
like shadows
through glass

riding gusty winds
northward

high over Lexington
it's getting chilly
don't want to be here

sailing warm breezes
over South Carolina
coastal pines

headed for Bermuda

too far – too far
a little panic

I'm back

drifting down
like a painted leaf
on a still autumn day

contact

the cage is locked

Upside Down

He Who Is Greatest

Ooooh – that root massage feels
good. I love the way you aerate
the soil, prepare dirt to hold more
water, consume death to regenerate life.

We tulips can't live without you. Your
stories are whispered in the wind; garbage
dump tales, recycled waste, castings
of black gold, food for the hungry.

Unassuming worm, you
have our praise for dexterity.
Though your work be hidden,
you are a servant to all.

The Whispering Veil

Beyond this world of visual beings
who gather in groups to practice litany,
deeper dimensions wait to be explored.

Liquid worlds limited only by our
vision and perception wait for
recognition so they can live again

in our lifetime. Sometimes in the twilight
hours a whisper in the air or a blurred
image penetrates the veil, only to be deleted
by monkeys of the mind.

Odoriferous Words

From the cesspool of seedy minds
repugnant words disguised as poetry
limp across the page,

words with a barnyard stench;
the horrid smells of hog pens, outhouses
and rotting garbage dumps defile

fresh clean air. Black on white
impressions linger in limbo,
repeat the sound of one leg walking.

Swinging on a Star

Her swing and sway
as she crossed the stage
could cause a man's
watch to stop, his
blood to sizzle;

a woman's too,
but for different reasons.

Her sultry song
rolled off her tongue
like a summer storm
beneath a clear blue sky.

Seventeen, queen
of the festival,
on her way to stardom.

I could only wonder how
hard it was going to be
to balance those beautiful
gifts, with all the ugly
they were going to attract.

Night School

Death came in a dream,

he stood in a beautiful
room by a huge table
adorned with delicious
food of every kind.

Overhead a banner read:

Welcome to Hell:
Home
of the Refresher Course

People bone thin and pale
walked in slow motion,
a strange sight indeed
with so much food.

The dinner bell rang
and all rushed to be seated,
only to find six-foot-long
eating utensils.

Spoons bumped, food splashed
over the table and dripped to the floor
as hungry mouths sucked
for nourishment.

Faster than light quells darkness
the dreamer stood in another
beautiful room, identical huge
table filled with delicious food,

robust people walked
with a spring in their step.

Overhead the sign read,

Welcome to Heaven:
An Introduction
to the Laws of Love

The dinner bell rang
and all gathered at the table
again to find eating utensils
six-feet-long.

After blessings were said, each
person dipped a spoon and fed
the person across the table.

Sources

On the walking trail, a honeybee
gyrated in circles, one wing hanging
limp, unable to lift into flight.

I stepped aside for fear I would
crush him; my mind began
to wander about his source of life.

Is his lifeline the same as mine,
or is he connected to some
unknown generator just for bees?

And what about the beetle, the bat,
the elephant with his long trunk,
and the giraffe with a six-foot neck?

Then there are those slithering snakes,
crocodiles with a mouth full of teeth,
and tiny little things that bite.

Do they all get life from a different
source, each one competing for
its moment on the giant screen, or

is it one source and all else
the art of survival, disrupted by ego?

The Great Divide

Gourmet food on silver platters
crystal glass and vintage wine.
Icons of a life that flatters,
cravings of the human kind.

Cold and hungry in an alley
one leg severed at the knee,
service rendered to his country
while fancy ladies met for tea.

When the battle cry is over
entrepreneurs distribute wealth.
When the soldier is left wanting
we expose our mental health.

Short Way Home

Beyond sensuality
we mount the air,
while feet still cling
to heavy clay.

Yet
we are not bound
by clouds of emotion
that swirl around us,

nor
by daunting yeas and nays
that do battle in our minds.

For soul
flies not on angel wings
but insightful realization,

and the shortest way home
is being there.

Folly on Ice

Rain forest – jewel of the earth,
pharmacy of the world, home
to two-thirds of all living things –
sucks carbon dioxide like a drunk
at a roadside beer hall. Now,
maimed by bulldozer, ax, fire.

Strike One.

White billows of smoke lift
skyward from tall brick stacks
as if stoked by the fires of hell.
Automobiles spew warm filth
into what once was pristine air,
ice slides from polar caps
as ocean waters rise.

Strike Two.

Governments struggling to be
world leaders haggle over air
quality and economics
while the common man vies
with nature for survival.

The pitcher winds, delivers.
It looks like a knuckle ball.

Hope

Dawn blinks on a mountaintop, below,
a fluffy white carpet of clouds drifts the valley.

Somewhere in an unseen hollow
the caw-caw-caw of a black crow
cracks still air, sounding reveille.
The earth stirs.

When first light streaks the horizon
painting thin cirrus clouds baby pink,
the magic moment arrives, and I revel
in the raw glory of a new day.

Elkmont Lights

In early June down at Elkmont
in the Great Smoky Mountain National Park
the fireflies blink in unison. People come
on crowded buses to watch the ten o'clock show.

Six blinks on, six seconds off, the forest
glows, the forest darkens. Spectators
stand transposed in silent wonder as nature
displays the power of working as one.

As I watch the syncopated rhythm, I begin
to ponder the lust of politics and religions to rule
the world, and I dream that someday they will learn
to synchronize their passions like the fireflies.

Searching for Light

Lying at peace on my bed
I ponder the words,

You must learn
not to be for or against;
take the middle path.

I stand aside, staring back
at my body.

Not knowing why,
I move about the house
looking inside electrical boxes,

black-and-white wires attached
to opposites sides of wall plugs
and switches stare back at me.

I jump back into my body
for a good night's sleep.

When morning eyes awaken
I flip the switch,

positive and negative forces
meet on neutral ground,

light fills the room
and questions are answered.

Take the middle path;
be the light bulb.

Revealed in a Dream

First cause – Part I

I stand in an ancient city in headdress
and chest armor with spear at the ready;
the hot sun gleams on temple spires
and scorches women in small wire cages.

I know not their crime, just that
they disobeyed the creed
and must be punished according
to laws dictated at the temple.

In her cage beside me she cries,
Let me out, please let me out;
but I stand in silent loyalty
to the High Priest's divine call.

In distant fields, I see woman
running for the woods, sometimes
a turncoat guard runs alongside;
he gave in, I kept the faith.

The moment we met
I knew I had to marry her,
I thought it to be love at first sight
until I analyzed the dream

then I knew we had karma.

The Rest of the Story

Transition – Part II

I held her hand in autumn's moonlight glow,
recalling vivid scenes of ages past;
how first it all began, I did not know,
just that it seem so right it had to last.

Many moons ago, a different time;
an ancient place, but subject to the now;
today our union forms a pantomime,
misgivings of past lives we disavow.

This life, we met to walk a student's path,
for karmic law recorded our past deeds;
repayment now requires an aftermath,
a life of trust that fortifies our creeds.

Romantic passion grew to avid trust,
replacing festered fears of long ago;
respect and understanding replaced lust,
relighting flames of hope that longed to grow.

We celebrate our fifty-second year,
devotion unobstructed by past tears.

Learning the Ways of Love

Restored – Part III

She said, *I love you for what you are.*
I wanted her to love me for what I could be.

I realized I might have to give
as much as I wished to receive
for love to happen.

So the journey began.

Fifty-three years passed, and I played tennis
this morning, took a nap this afternoon,
and now I sit here writing this poem

while she talks on the phone to one of our
two grown daughters about how our three
teenage grandchildren are doing in school.

Every now and then, she looks over and asks,
Are you ready to take me to dinner now?

Color of Love

From afar,

two dark silhouettes
bathed in morning mist
on a deserted beach.

As the gap closes,
silver hair,
wrinkled brown skin
comes into view.

Fingers locked,
bare feet splashing,
they laugh and giggle
in childlike play.

Suddenly the rainbow!

An aura of blue-green
fading to golden-red
connects heads and shoulders.

Stunned, yet fearful
of disrupting such magic,
I nod in passing,
whisper, *good morning.*

I walked on, knowing
I had just witnessed
the true color of love.

First Snowfall

Purple finches fight for space
at the safflower feeder, doves and sparrows
search for fallen seeds on the ground, titmouse
and blue jay crunch sunflower seed.

Starlings fight over suet in a wire
basket, red birds, chickadees and pigeons
line electrical wires, awaiting their chance
to join the party.

A downy woodpecker flies in to assess
his odds of getting to the suet basket, but,
more timid, he cowers until a larger
red belly joins him, and the starlings flee.

Pigeons, tired of waiting on wires,
land with a great flutter of wings,
take control of the ground. Doves and
sparrows scatter to trees.

Mimicking a shopping mall at Christmas, birds
push, grab, and fight for seeds. Why such a state
of panic, why had everyone come to feed
simultaneously?

In the west, sky darkens, snow mixed with
freezing rain flies on crisp northerly winds.
The birds had tuned in to a global meteorologist.

Easy Picking

Each morning
when songbirds
disperse the night
and wake the day,

when golden sunrays
light eastern skies
with yellow,
orange and red,

a great blue heron
flies over on his way
to a fishing hole
down at the creek.

Today he detoured
over a neighbor's house
where he suddenly
descended into a
bubbling water garden.

He took up a position
near a jagged rock
surrounded by purple
hyacinth, a safe haven
for fantailed goldfish.

He lingered the morning,
just savoring the gold.

Entwined

The small and large,
universally entwined,
move in synchronized
harmony like a symphony.

How do we fathom
that which is too large
to absorb, too small
to imagine?

Should we study every
action so as not to
disrupt what we do not
fully understand?

Who will pay
the price if we abuse
the resources entrusted
to our care?

What will be the cost
should we fail
to hold reverence
for life?

Naked Truth

We had the sauna all to ourselves,
he and I.

Wrapped in towels,
perspiration streamed
down naked skin.

He inquired of my age, then
proceeded to explain he
was three years older.

If we knew long ago
what we know now, we would have
done a lot of things different, he quipped.

You're right; we learn from experience,
and by the time we have been around
long enough to know what's happening,
we're too old to do anything about it;

makes me want to know the purpose of it all,
I replied.

Oh, but there is purpose, he said with a wink,
I firmly believe the Bible is the word of God.

What do you make of the scripture
that says the sons of God saw the daughters
of men and took them as wives, and their
sons were men of renown? I ask.

Ah…ah…I…I haven't really read it all,
I…I'm not a Bible scholar, he stuttered.
We sat in silence for a while before
he rose with a smile and said,

Have a good day.

Take care, I replied.

My Father and the Book

Saturday afternoons my father always read
The Book. He never questioned The Book,
he just called it the Word of God. He talked
about Adam, Eve, and that snake, how Cain
killed Abel and fled to the land of Nod,

took a wife. I always wondered
who created that other woman.

Drinking was a sin, but my father liked
the story of Jesus turning water into
wine. Never said, if wine was a sin,
why Jesus didn't just purify the water.

He died at ninety-three,
still trying through failed eyes
to read The Book.

Alone in the Cattails

Down by the lake this morning,
trees stood on their heads
in a smooth mirror of water,

among reeds and cattails
a Red-winged Blackbird searched
for a safe haven to build a nest.

Every now and then he flew to the top
of a reed to sing, *sweeeet, sweeet, sweeet,*
but his mate did not answer, so he continued
to search and sing the morning long.

Spring, just around the corner,
it was time to get on with
making love and nesting.

Where could she be? Had some wayward
wind blown her off course on her way
to their nesting grounds, or had some
shiny-feathered, slick rooster seduced her?

Circle of Life

A universe with purpose
designed in circles:

round moons circle
planets that circle
stars that circle

the center of a galaxy
that circles some
unknown source
too far to know.

Seasons moving in circles
bring chance for new
life to the earth. Circles
on the ground, circles
in the sky,

why would I think
my life to be but one
straight line?

If Only

Adam and Eve
had not had sex or eaten
that apple or whatever
forbidden fruit caused
mankind to veer off
in the wrong direction
Cain would not have killed Abel
Noah would not have built an ark
the children of Israel would not
have been slaves in Egypt
the Red Sea would not have parted
Jesus would not have had to take
time out to come to earth
Christmas would not have stolen Saturnalia
there would have been no inquisitions
no crusades or witch burning
the Trail of Tears and Wounded Knee
horrors would not have happened
World War II would not be in the history books
the atom bomb would never have exploded
Hitler would be a nice guy
televangelism would not be a thriving
business and nine-eleven would be
just another day on the calendar.

Makes me want to give up sex
and stop eating apples.

Holy Makeover

With the grace of a saint,
she hovers over the waiting
room at Catholic Hospital.

Her toe-length, white gown complements
the baby blue scarf draping head and shoulders.
Only a lock of reddish-blonde hair exposed,

her creamy complexion a perfect
match to the fair-haired
infant she cradles in her arms.

With head bowed, her eyes fall
upon the child, an enchanting statue:
Irish lass with newborn baby.

I wonder where in the Holy Land
her birth might have occurred.

A Walk in the Park

As I locked the car and began my morning walk, a woman
and her leashed pit bull jumped ahead; the dog tossed
me an ugly look. I slowed to give them plenty of space.

Picking up candy wrappers and drink cups, I
made my way toward the pond where four men
teed off in a game of disc golf.

Each man tried to sail his disc across
the pond's narrow end rather than
around trees to find the wire basket.

Four turtles sunning on a log raised their heads to laugh
as the saucers sailed low over water; three discs made
it to the far bank, the last one took a bath with the fish.

On down the paved path a disoriented earthworm
wiggled his last wiggle on the warm blacktop.

I gave him a gentle lift and placed him in the shady
damp grass, his wiggle increasing as if to say, *Thank You!*

Down where the dirt trail veers to woodlands,
I met two swallowtail butterflies dancing on air
over a patch of yellow buttercups; circling wide,
I avoided intrusion into their mating ritual.

As I entered the woods two mockingbirds competed
for air time as if they were contestants on *American Idol.*
Deeper in to the woods, while watching two robins scurry
for worms, I realized there was no litter on the dirt path,

a clear sign that those who cherish dirt fields and woodlands see
Mother Earth differently than those who revel in asphalt and steel.

Morning in the Park

Hard to find a parking place, soccer
moms and dads line fields shouting
encouragement to their twelve-year-old

children, stand to cheer when red or blue
scores a goal. Close by on a small knoll,
practitioners of the art of fencing

and medieval swordsmanship display
ancient skills. On down the walking trail,
beyond the white oak grove, a more subdued

group waits to tee off in a weekend
regional disc golf tournament where
yellow, orange, and chartreuse discs

sail around treetops and fly over bushes
in search of wire baskets. Across a concrete
bridge down by the pond, a green bullfrog

sits in solitude, waiting for the next wayward
insect to grace his lightning quick tongue.

Life on the Flip Side

What if what we think we know
is in reverse, and left is right
and right is left, what if pictures
in our mind are like reflections
in a mirror, what if the sun
does not really rise and set?

What if negative is not bad,
but simply the pen with which we
write our story on the pages of life,
and what if darkness is the only
door into light?

What if love is faster than light
and arrives before it starts,
with a sound that echoes louder
than thunder?

What if God is not love,
but Love is God and does not
sit on a heavenly throne
waiting to be praised but
lies silently within each of us,
waiting to be recognized?

Part II

Say It
Upside Down:
Nonets in Reflection

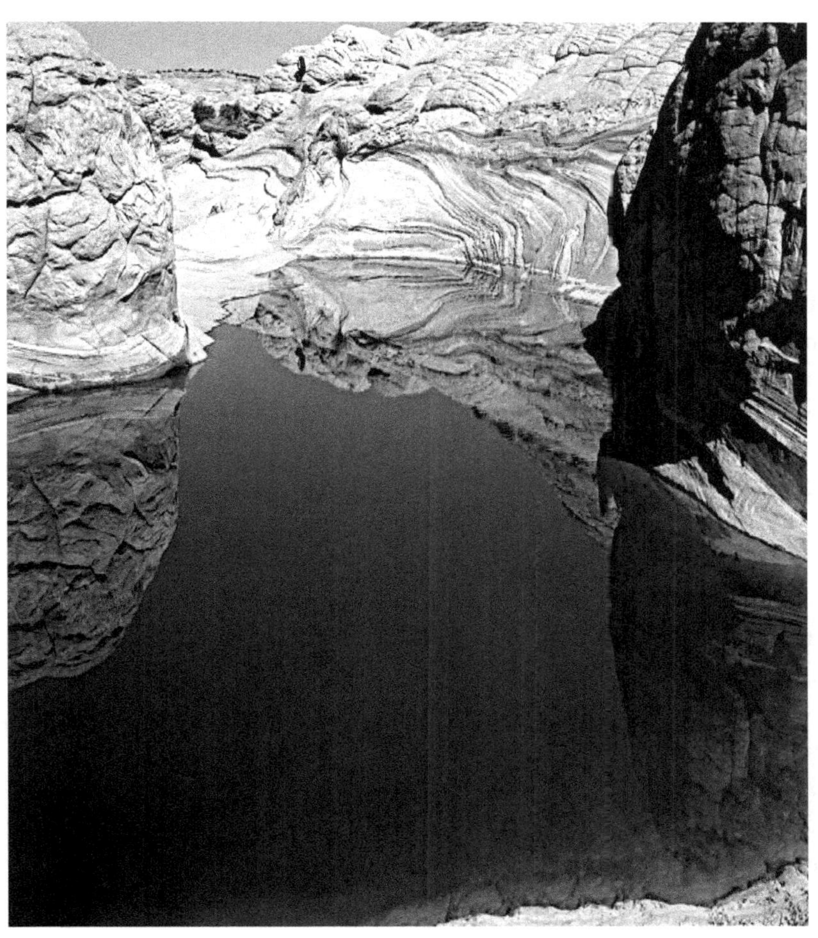

Light in reflection
Projects a different viewpoint
Turns life upside down

The Beginning

Fresh from the womb, I nursed Mother's breast.
Nothing better than genuine.
Life starts with exuberance:
four sisters, one brother,
my mother, forty.
I was unplanned,
and welcomed
tender
care.

Care,
tender
and welcomed.
I was unplanned,
my mother forty.
Four sisters, one brother:
life starts with exuberance.
Nothing better than genuine.
Fresh from the womb, I nursed Mother's breast.

Reflections

Twilight of one life mirrors the next,
a reflection of lessons learned.
Footprints left for tomorrow,
a road never ending.
Higher view ahead,
steep hills to climb;
with each step
upward,
light.

Light
upward,
with each step:
steep hills to climb,
higher view ahead.
A road never ending,
footprints left for tomorrow.
A reflection of lessons learned,
twilight of one life mirrors the next.

Shadows of the Past

Shadows of sunset stretch before me,
short rays of sunrise remembered.
In the evening of my day
each moment of the past
reflected, limpid.
Naked ahead,
grey twilight
fades to
dark.

Dark
fades to
grey twilight.
Naked ahead
reflected limpid,
each moment of the past.
In the evening of my day,
short rays of sunrise remembered.
Shadows of sunset stretch before me.

Searching for Now

As awareness peels away darkness,
a layered soul unfolds to light.
Like a snake discards its skin,
old habits fade away,
new visions appear.
Purpose regained,
higher ground
in view
now.

Now
in view
higher ground,
purpose regained.
New visions appear,
old habits fade away
like a snake discards its skin.
A layered soul unfolds to light
as awareness peels away darkness.

Renewed Life

Birds and flowers celebrate new life,
southern wind renews spirit's song.
Turtles bask in noonday sun,
daffodils, raise your heads;
resurrect morning.
Destination
off center:
rewrite
now.

Now,
rewrite
off-center
destination.
Resurrect morning
daffodils, raise your heads;
turtles, bask in noonday sun.
Southern wind renews spirit's song.
Birds and flowers celebrate new life.

Migrations

A mockingbird sings the new day's song,
fledgling robins posed to migrate.
The maple tree longs for green,
awaiting new pigment.
Day and night balance;
Season's cycle
renewing
winter
cold.

Cold
winter
renewing
season's cycle,
day and night balance.
Awaiting new pigment,
the maple tree longs for green.
Fledgling robins posed to migrate,
a mockingbird sings the new day's song.

Music

When words vibrate across human minds,
a rush of music fills the heart.
Energy renews body,
creative fluids flow,
revived visions flash.
The world expands,
dark shadows
recede
now.

Now
recede
dark shadows!
The world expands,
revived visions flash,
creative fluids flow,
energy renews body.
A rush of music fills the heart
when words vibrate in the human mind.

Morning Song

Waves pound rocky shores with rhythmic splash.
Seagulls synchronize approval,
lend music to the morning.
Wind's overture answers
with feather soft breeze.
In salty air,
Black Terns fly
wave-top
smooth.

Smooth,
wave-top
Black Terns fly
in salty air.
With feather soft breeze
wind's overture answers,
lends music to the morning.
Seagulls synchronize approval,
waves pound rocky shores with rhythmic splash.

Mourning

Red on pink like blood on stucco walls,
cut flowers–tears in a bottle.
Essence of life surrendered
in the height of glory.
Goodbye lonely days;
butterfly wings,
honeybees.
Welcome
death.

Death
welcomes
honeybees,
butterfly wings;
goodbye lonely days.
In the height of glory,
essence of life surrendered.
Cut flowers–tears in a bottle,
red on pink like blood on stucco walls.

Mingled Shades

Light mingles with night in twilight shade,
slumber regenerates spirit,
echoes life's best yesterdays,
greets dreams of tomorrow;
a fresh new viewpoint
expands choices.
Morning sun
renews
hope.

Hope
renews
morning sun,
expands choices.
A fresh new viewpoint
greets dreams of tomorrow,
echoes life's best yesterdays.
Slumber regenerates spirit;
light mingles with night in twilight shade.

Mind Shadows

From dank, darkened minds, crafty words spew
as poison darts fly through blowguns.
Usurped by aggrandizement,
ego craves attention
without compromise.
Consistently,
calm virtue
whispers,
wait.

Wait!
whispers
calm virtue.
Consistently,
without compromise,
ego craves attention,
usurped by aggrandizement.
As poison darts fly through blow guns,
from dank, darkened minds, crafty words spew.

Mind Games

Psychology–monkeys of the mind
astutely swinging phrase to phrase,
like words in a computer:
punch to add or delete,
shift to rearrange.
Bold swift action,
make changes,
review,
save.

Save,
review,
make changes.
Bold swift action,
shift to rearrange
punch to add or delete.
Like words in a computer,
astutely swinging phrase to phrase;
psychology–monkeys of the mind.

Manifestations

Creative essence manifesting,
new laws sing to perceptive souls,
form to their own expression.
Pure spirit's gift bestowed,
flows through open minds:
thoughts that texture,
molding hands,
guiding
life.

Life,
guiding
molding hands:
thoughts that texture
flow through open minds.
Pure spirit's gift bestowed,
forms to its own expression.
New laws sing to perceptive souls,
creative essence manifesting.

Left Behind

Rearview mirror wet with misty tears,
success and failure, black on white.
Rainbows circle in the mind,
add texture to shadows.
Pain, like lifting weights,
produces strength.
Awareness,
brings soul
light.

Light
brings soul
awareness,
produces strength.
Pain, like lifting weights,
adds textures to shadows.
Rainbows circle in the mind,
success and failure black on white,
rearview mirror wet with misty tears.

In Tune

A single note in Creation's song,
celestial universal sound:
I'm syncopated rhythm,
rhyme free metered to beat.
Oratorios,
obbligatos,
concertos,
await
now.

Now
awaits
concertos,
obbligatos,
oratorios.
Rhyme, free metered to beat,
I'm syncopated rhythm,
celestial universal sound:
a single note in Creation's song.

Holy Rerun

While Christmas bells ring throughout the mall,
bombs burst in rugged mountain towns,
terrorists train to slaughter,
replaying holy wars.
Hate from ages old:
crusades that squash,
swords that maim,
pretend
love.

Love
pretends
swords that maim,
crusades that squash.
Hate from ages old
replaying holy wars,
terrorists train to slaughter.
Bombs burst in rugged mountain towns
while Christmas bells ring throughout the mall.

History of War

Dawn of humankind records first war,
perpetual in today's world.
Bespattered in history:
political conflicts,
suicide bombers.
Religions reign:
terror's son
promotes
fear.

Fear
promotes
terror's son:
religions reign.
Suicide bombers,
political conflicts,
bespattered in history.
Perpetual in today's world,
dawn of mankind records first war.

Growing Up

Baseball–basketball–horseshoes, my game:
fishing and girls on radar screen.
Started while still in high school,
stopped work at sixty-five.
Hard, dual lesson learned
through yin and yang.
Uncovered,
footprints
faint.

Faint
footprints
uncovered
through yin and yang,
hard dual lesson learned.
Stopped work at sixty-five,
started while still in high school.
Fishing and girls on radar screen;
baseball–basketball–horseshoes, my game.

Getting Published

Half of four bits is twenty-five cents,
ten times a quarter, two fifty.
I divide or multiply;
cultivating rewards
I falter in fear.
Planting to reap,
I publish
my self
true.

True,
my self
I publish.
Planting to reap,
I falter in fear.
Cultivating rewards,
I divide or multiply;
ten times a quarter, two fifty,
half of four bits is twenty-five cents.

Which Star is Mine?

Who am I–what could my purpose be?
Am I worthy of life's treasures,
can I face my darkest night,
reflect bright morning light,
find motif within?
Which star is mine
in heaven's
sparkling
glow?

Glow,
sparkling
in heaven.
Which star is mine?
Find motif within,
reflect bright morning light:
can I face my darkest night,
am I worthy of life's treasures?
Who am I–what could my purpose be?

Expanded View

The ensemble of life, extended
beyond the eye – removed from touch.
Germs too small for detection,
galaxies veiled to mind:
above and below
worlds expanding;
strings in tune,
vibrate
life.

Life
vibrates,
strings in tune.
Worlds expanding
above and below,
galaxies veiled to mind,
germs too small for detection.
Beyond the eye – removed from touch,
the ensemble of life extended.

Educated Awareness

Knowledge – black on white words in a book.
Wisdom found through application:
experience the teacher,
latch onto the message.
Soul's eternal quest:
enlightenment,
awareness,
basic
truth.

Truth,
basic
awareness,
enlightenment:
soul's eternal quest.
Latch onto the message,
experience the teacher.
Wisdom – found through application.
Knowledge – black on white words in a book.

Contemplation

When monkeys of the mind are quiet,
windows open to spirit's eye.
Heartstrings chant music divine.
Soul's radiant beams cast
ethereal lights,
dance in rhythm.
Eternal
rainbows
sing.

Sing,
rainbows
eternal!
Dance in rhythm,
ethereal lights.
Soul's radiant beams cast
heartstrings, chant music divine.
Windows open to spirit's eye
when monkeys of the mind are quiet.

Chef's Delight

Hand picked fresh mushrooms, delectable,
cooked in sauce with Salisbury steak.
Some full of deadly poison:
don't make a dumb mistake.
Beneath the button,
cut off the stem,
to count spores.
Scrumptious
gem.

Gem,
scrumptious.
To count spores,
cut off the stem
beneath the button;
don't make a dumb mistake.
Some full of deadly poison.
Cooked in sauce with Salisbury steak,
hand picked fresh mushrooms delectable.

Assumptions

I must imagine I know nothing,
to open life to everything.
Continuing my journey,
I seek wisdom within.
Unproved faith is void,
reality:
cleansed by truth,
exists
now.

Now
exists,
cleansed by truth:
reality.
Unproved faith is void.
I seek wisdom within.
Continuing my journey
to open life to everything,
I must imagine I know nothing.

Silent Sound

Positive thinking creates action,
releases power of the mind,
brings clarity to mission,
calms emotional tides,
inspires awareness.
Soft stillness reigns,
life renews
tranquil
peace.

Peace
tranquil:
life renews.
Soft stillness reigns,
inspires awareness,
calms emotional tides,
brings clarity to mission,
releases power of the mind.
Positive thinking creates action.

Experiencing Now

Being trapped in life's busy days' rush
robs soul of now experience:
turns peace into contention,
interrupts new vision,
spawns anxiety.
Mind in turmoil,
naked nerves
rubbing
now.

Now,
rubbing
naked nerves.
Mind in turmoil
spawns anxiety:
interrupts new vision,
turns peace into contention,
robs soul of now experience,
being trapped in life's busy days' rush.

Beyond Books

An ardent heart is an open door
to creativity's lighthouse,
my own solemn adventure
into a world of dreams.
Where lies my true self?
Without teachers,
beyond books;
the real
me?

Me,
the real,
beyond books
without teachers,
where lies my true self.
Into a world of dreams,
my own solemn adventure
to creativity's lighthouse.
An ardent heart is an open door.

Part III

Say It
in Micro
with
Cinquains

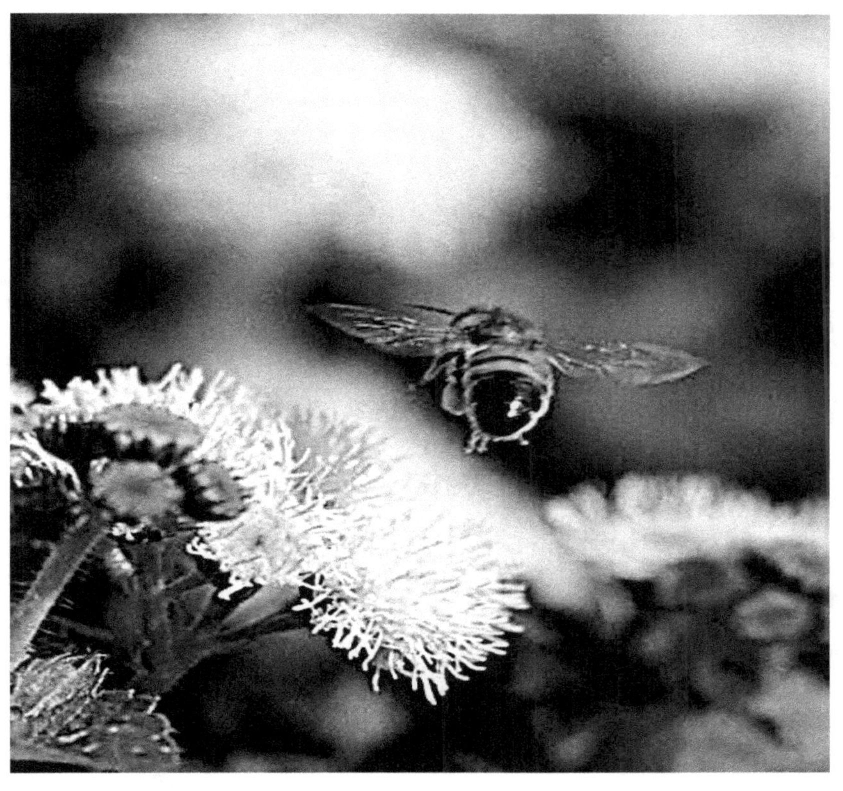

Tiny honeybee
Pollinator of nature
Sipping sweet nectar

Writing in Form

Cinquain

No wasted sounds

Every word to the point

Like an arrow zipped from a bow

Target

Yearning

Romance

Fiddles on strings

Of my heart's emotions

Hope tickles valentine desires

First love

Twilight

Pink clouds

Blue sky background

Light's last glossy glimmer

Another day's experience

Painted

Tides of Time

Wisdom

Like ocean waves

Flooding sandy beaches

Surveys minds for retention pools

High tide

Transition

Springtime
Dogwoods blooming
Blue eggs fill robin's nest
Chorus frogs sing in unison
New life

Summer
Turtles on log
Bare feet splashing in mud
Fruit and grain ripen in the sun
Sustained

Autumn
North wind blows cold
Night swallows warm sunrays
Falling leaves paint land yellow-red
Transit

Winter
Bleak and frosty
Blowing snow, freezing rain
Life retreats to hibernation
At rest

Vernal
Flowers and bees
Songbirds sing harmony
Life force sparks rejuvenation
Renewed

New life
Flowers and bees
Bare feet splashing in mud
Falling leaves paint land yellow red
At rest

The Beginning

Woman

Magic garden

Mysterious fruit tree

Talking snake hisses persuasion

First sin

Afterglow

Wisdom

Beams like sunshine

Refracts in open minds

Fills willing hearts with enticing

Rainbows

Style

Deep thought

Rare in public

Conformity to norm

Fear of rejection consumes minds

Vision

Ahoy! Ahoy!

Noah

Builder of boats

Zookeeper on high seas

Protector of wild animals

Captain

Summer Turmoil

Storm clouds

Lightning flashes

Strong wind chases thunder

Like the devil pursuing soul

Restless

Summer Sounds

August

Cicada sings

In evening's twilight glow

Light gives way to shadow–nightfall

Peace reigns

Soul in Motion

Music

Vibrates within

Tiny strings sing life's song

Harmonic sound lifts soul higher

Sweet peace

Life's Song

Laughter

Music of soul

Energizes brain cells

Aligns heart's beat to life's rhythm

Complete

Shadows

Twilight

Like dawn's first light

Denotes a change in time

Night and day mix–exchange places

Silk smooth

December 21, 2012

Black hole

Deep space magnet

Galactic alignment

Last day on Mayan calendar

New age

School Days

Earthlings

All souls equal

Kids experiencing

Creator's elementary

Classroom

Revelations

Darkness

Reveals the moon

Exposes distant stars

Night affirms content of the day

Unfeigned

Revealed

Beauty

Ugly unmasked

Spirit void of facade

Soul prepared for graduation

New wings

Renewal

Nightfall

Evening's last glow

Starlight peeps through darkness

Another cycle completed

Placid

Poet's Pen

God's poem

Laid to the ground

Boiled to pulp and spread thin

Inscribed with ink from poet's pen

Pine tree

Physical

Earthbound

Tied to the wheel

Circling–struggling–hoping

Unable to loose binding chains

Vise grip

People's Choice

Conflict

Left versus right

Politicians battle

Each party waving its own flag

Stalemate

Path to Light

Wisdom

In dark of night

Reflects in morning light

Eyes open to understanding

Divine

One is Many

White light

Rainbow adorned

Enlarges eye's spectrum

A multitude of rays beaming

One source

Morning

Whispers

Light plays on fog

Silent sound clings to earth

Music of songbirds vibrating

Serene

Mind Power

Visions

Mind photographs

Soul's imaginations

Creating good and evil forms

Future

Love versus Love

Mock love

Raw emotion

Feigns desired promise

True love expectations revised

Canceled

Mind Passions

Lustful
Uncontrolled want
Cravings of the body
Pulse of soul devoured by passions
Hunger

Anger
Raw rage unleashed
Passion out of control
A disease eating at the heart
Decay

Greedy
Wanton desire
Unfettered ambition
Mind warped with appetite for more
Consumed

Ego
Running on high
Brash vanity unchecked
Soul lost in self-created fog
Pompous

Attached
To illusions
Holding to stale ideas
In fear of new understanding
Bondage

Hunger
Wanton desire
Passion out of control
Soul lost in self-created fog
Attached

Libido

Raw lust

Primitive mind

A ball and chain to soul

Consumes creative energy

Dead end

In Vain

Ego

Inflated self

Primal gross vanity

Fanning hot emotional flames

Ashes

House of Mystery

Brothers

Cain killed Abel

Fled to the land of Nod

Took unto himself a woman

Puzzle

Heartache

Misled

She gave her love

And her body to him

Now alone–pregnant with his child

She weeps

Freedom

Wisdom

Enlightenment

Gained through experience

Soul's pathway to pure worlds of light

Unchained

For My Country

Outcast

Mind and body

Surrendered in war's hell

People pass by–soldier unseen

Denied

Listening to Life

Heart songs

Mental music

Awareness live on stage

Consciousness reaching for new heights

Freedom

Full Moon

Nightfall

Orange glow casts

Shadows over the land

A sure sign that beyond the dark

There's light

Eye Contact

Concepts

In fear's mirror

Yield black and white pictures

Viewed through the clear prism of love

Rainbows

Evil's Sword

Fear's claw

Deadly poison

Contaminates soul's love

Decimates creativity

Cripples

Evaluating Worth

Value

Weighed on life's scale

Mind sees blessing received

Clueless that life counts gifts given

Viewpoint

Energy Pill

Laughter

Pure remedy

For life's provocateurs

Elevates awareness of soul

Rewards

Earth Virus

River

Poison water

Flowing to the blue sea

Man-made toxic gases rising

Think green

Dusk

Peaceful

Light receding

Dark swallows light's last rays

Evening's silence sound – work complete

My time

Death

Cold clay

Reclaims its own

Old body recycled

Death but a comma in life's book

Untold

Common Sense

Dreaming

World of respect

Angry war cravings past

Mankind elevates to new heights

Awake

Choose Hope

Fear's tears

Religion's hell

Politician's dogma

Designed to control human thought

Cut rope

At the Gallery

Artist

Of confusion

Dead fish on tan canvas

Contemplating a work of art

Spilled paint

Avoid the Snare

Evil

Lying in wait

Setting trappings of fear

I refuse his offer of war

Freedom

Change

My mind

Open to change

My heart to peace and joy

When the trials of life weigh me down

There's love

Part IV

Say It
with Questions
in a Letter

It ain't those parts of the Bible that I can't understand that bother me, it's the parts that I do understand.

– Mark Twain

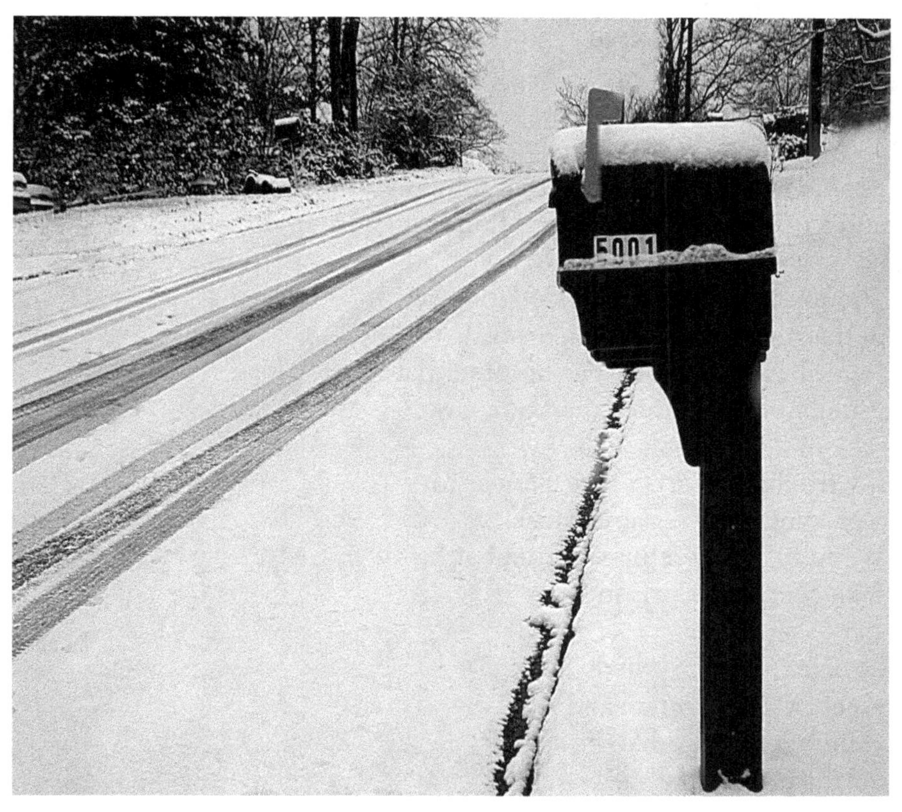

Letters in the mail
On a cold, snowy morning
Hoping for answers

Letters to the Lord – I
Children

Dear Lord,

I come with a troubled heart, a mind filled with guilt
and a plea for answers to questions that burden my soul.

Though I have procrastinated for years
in the study of Your written word,
I now hasten to read Your book so that
I might better understand Your ways.

My troubled heart comes from a story
regarding Your servant, Moses.
When his army returned from battle
with Midianites prisoners,

he ordered all be killed
except virgin women and girl
children; they were to be spared
for the pleasure of the warriors.

Lord, the boy children, did You
cast them into the lake of fire?
I pray that You let them live if only
as household servants for Your chosen.

My guilt manifested when I read
that if anyone has stubborn children
they should present them to the
elders of the city to be stoned to death.

Lord, I have two stubborn children,
but I didn't know about this law until today.
Is it too late? If I have them stoned,
should my grandchildren be stoned also?

Letters to the Lord – II
Zoo Ark

As I continue to read Your book,
questions arise about Noah and the ark.

The ark, 300 cubits (500 ft.) in length,
50 cubits (84 ft.) in breadth,
30 cubits (50 ft.) in height,
divided into three (16-17 ft.) stories.

Lord, some giraffes are 20 ft. tall;
were any special arrangements made?
Unclean animals went in by twos,
clean animals by sevens. How much
hay, how much meat, did it take to feed
the animals for ten months?

Was there a place to store the meat
and keep the polar bears cool?
If the animals came to Noah, did
the American Basin swim the Atlantic?

Were cages aboard to keep the birds
away from insects? How were the large
meat eaters separated from small animals?
Could Satan have sneaked aboard,
disguised as a snake?

When all were aboard, you shut them in.
Considering all the animal waste,
how was the boat kept clean?

The water rose 15 cubits (25 ft.)
above the mountains and destroyed
every living substance. What did the animals
eat when they left the ark?

Lord, that's all I have for now;
when I get more questions, I'll write again.

Letters to the Lord – III
Forbidden Fruit

Dear Lord,

I read Your creation story again today,
and the part where Adam and Eve
ate the forbidden fruit
causes me concerns for my diet.

Some refer to the forbidden fruit
as the apple. I think it's a metaphor
for sex, because the story says:

And the eyes of them both were
opened, and they knew they were
naked; and they sewed fig leaves
together, and made themselves aprons.

If the apple was forbidden
and it contains the secret knowledge,
I should be getting smarter
since I eat apples every day.

If sex was the forbidden fruit,
were You repenting when
You said, *Be fruitful*, and *multiply?*

Lord, if it was apples, is it still a sin
to eat them? Is it all apples, or just
certain kinds?

If it was sex, I pray that You have taken
it off the forbidden list, for many of us
have been fruitful.

Please Lord,
answer soon so I will know whether
to give up sex or stop eating apples.

Letters to the Lord – IV
Before and After

Dear Lord,

You said to Jeremiah,

Before I formed thee in the belly
I knew thee;...

The souls You know before birth,
do they survive death?

Do they join sperm and egg at conception,
or is it more like ordering a car
and waiting until after delivery
to take the driver's seat?

Letters to the Lord – V
Giant Sons

Dear Lord,

I continue to read Your book,
and I am a little confused.
I would like to ask more questions.

How many sons do You have?

I read in one part of Your book
Jesus of Nazareth was Your only son.
Yet, in another place,

Your word says that more than one
of Your sons came to earth,
took wives, and their children were
men of renown.

If this is true, what were their names?

How many grandchildren do You have?

The story says there were giants in those days;
were any of Your sons or grandsons giants?

Could the giant David killed have been
one of Your great, great grandsons?

Letters to the Lord – VI

Sun, Stand Still

Dear Lord,

Joshua said,
Sun, stand thou still upon Gibeon;
and thou, moon, in the valley of Ajalon.

Were these Your instructions, or was Joshua
trying to incite his people to rise up
against the Amorites?

Lord, did the sun revolve
around the earth in those days,
or was Joshua just unaware?

As the solar system works now,
the sun rises and sets
due to the earth's rotation.

Lord, to get the described results,
am I wrong in thinking Joshua would
have had to tell the earth to stand still?

Letters to the Lord – VII

Born Again

Dear Lord,

Once again, I write to You
because I have failed to understand.

Followers of Jesus teach
that a person is born, has one life
to become a believer, and is forever
rewarded based on choices made.

You told Jeremiah
You knew him before
he was formed in the womb.

If we exist before we are incarnated,
can we be reincarnated?

My confusion increased; Jesus
told his disciples John the Baptist
was Elias returned.

If John lived before as Elias,
was Jesus teaching reincarnation?

Letters to the Lord – VIII

Standing on the Corner

Dear Lord

In Your book,
John says he saw four angels standing
on four corners of the earth,
holding four winds.

Satellite pictures from space
show earth to be a sphere
like game-balls we play with.

I have played baseball, basketball and tennis;
I cannot find corners on any of these balls.
This indicates to me that our planet
does not have corners.

Lord,
was John speaking of a future time
when the earth would be flattened
into a square with four corners,

or was he seeing *through a glass darkly?*

Letters to the Lord – IX

False Prophets

Dear Lord,

I am trying to understand the work of prophets.

Ahaz, King of Judah, occupied Jerusalem;
Rezin, King of Syria, and Remaliah, King of Israel,
marched on Jerusalem to make war.
You sent Isaiah to Ahaz saying not to fear,
You would give a sign.

Therefore the Lord himself shall give you a sign;
Behold, a virgin shall conceive, and bear a son,
and shall call his name Immanuel.

Isaiah went unto the prophetess, and she conceived;
the child was named Mahershalalhashbaz.
Was Isaiah the father, is that why the name was changed?
Anyway, Isaiah's prophecy did not come true.
Rezin and Remaliah defeated Ahaz,
carried him off to Damascus.

Your book says:
When a prophet speaketh in the name of the Lord,
if the thing follow not, nor come to pass,
that is the thing which the Lord hath not spoken,
but the prophet hath spoken it presumptuously:
thou shall not be afraid of him.

Lord,
was Isaiah a false prophet?

Letters to the Lord – X
Rewrite

Dear Lord,

Some stories in your book
are copies of older stories.

In the book of Matthew,
Isaiah's prophecy to Ahaz is retold,
attributing the virgin birth to Mary.
Again, the child was to be called Immanuel,
but the name given was Yehoshua / Yeshua
a.k.a. Jesus.

Matthew said an angel appeared to Joseph
to make the announcement,
Luke said the angel appeared to Mary.
Mark and John were silent on the subject.

King Herod ordered all children
two and under destroyed. An angel warned
Joseph to flee to Egypt; when Herod died,
the angel instructed Joseph to take mother
and child back to Israel.

Lord, what happened to John the Baptist;
how did he escape the slaughter? Why
did the angel not warn his father to flee?

Letters to the Lord – XI
Creation of Man

Dear Lord,

I can't get the creation story
out of my mind, so many questions.

After night, day, fish, animals,
You made man in Your own image.

If we are in Your image,
why are we not perfect?
Did the DNA fail?

Satan, disguised as a snake
escaped from a bottomless pit.

Why didn't you seal the pit,
or better yet, just zap him?

Why not zap Adam and Eve
also, make the flood unnecessary,
start all over before the earth
became populated?

Lord,
was the DNA flaw part of the plan,
or just an oversight?

Letters to the Lord – XII

Dual Fathers

Dear Lord,

In Matthew Your book traces the genealogy
of King David down to Jesus, son of Mary,
twenty-eight generations. Again the genealogy
is traced in Luke, listing forty-three generations.

The Luke story says Jesus was son of Joseph.
Matthew says the Holy Ghost fathered Jesus.

Lord, only the names David, Joseph, and Jesus
are included in both genealogies. If the two accounts
distort truth, or, if Joseph was not the father,
isn't the chain to King David broken?

Letters to the Lord – XIII

Tabloid News

Dear Lord,

I write today about stories of murder,
deceit, slavery, incest, rape, annihilation,
terrorists, and fathers sleeping with daughters,
all carried out by heroes found in Your book.

A king takes three hundred wives,
woman gives maidservant to bear
husband's child, animals are burned
in Your honor.

Lord, help me understand;
these stories are headlines fit
for the tabloid newspapers
rather than a church marquee.

Yet the church says
they are Your words, revelation
given to Your servants and written
in the Holy Bible.

Please Lord, tell me it's not true.

Letters to the Lord – XIV

Right to Choose

Dear Lord,

Abortion or right to choose? Those who speak most dramatically in Your name declare abortion in any form to be murder, even to save the mother's life. Some extend their view to stem cell research, a potential cure for diseases that destroy mind and body. Many who believe choice is between a woman and her doctor extend their views to late-term pregnancy.

I have been reading for answers to these questions in Your book. Joshua, at Your command, committed genocide against seven different communities of people. He smote them with the sword, he *let none remain*. Were any of the women *with child?* If so, did he consider the fetus?

Lord, is it more virtuous to kill mother and child than to abort a fetus? What about the enemies' newborn; is it okay to kill them?

Please answer soon Lord, for we continue to fight wars.

Letters to the Lord – XV

Judgment Day

Dear Lord,

In Your book, Jesus describes a time of tribulation.

Brother will betray brother to death, and father the son,
and children shall rise up against parents, and shall
cause them to be put to death.

The abomination of desolation warns people
to flee to the mountains, not to return home
to gather garments, woe to them that are with child.

After the tribulation the sun will be darkened
the moon will not give its light, stars of heaven shall fall.

And then shall they see the Son of man coming
in the clouds with great power and glory.

And then shall he send his angels, and shall gather
together his elect from the four winds, from the uttermost
part of the earth to the uttermost part of heaven.

In conclusion, Jesus says: *Verily I say unto you,*
that this generation shall not pass, till all these things be done.

And again Jesus says: *Verily I say unto you,*
there be some standing here, which shall
not taste of death, until they see the Son of man
coming in his kingdom.

Generations have passed and history has no record
of the sun being darkened, the moon not giving light,
stars falling from heaven or the Son of man coming
in clouds or angels gathering Your elect from the four winds.

Lord, did Jesus get the time wrong, did the words get edited,
or did You decide to change the schedule?

Letters to the Lord – XVI

Born Sinners

Dear Lord,

According to the creation story, first came Adam,
then from his rib, Eve, and then there were two.
Eve gave birth to Cain and Abel, and there were four.
Cain killed Abel, then there were three.
Cain fled to Nod, took a wife, and there were four.

Lord, this is where I get confused and questions arise.
We are taught by those who speak in Your name
that because Adam and Eve sinned, we are all
born as sinners and must be saved to escape hell.

Cain's wife was not a child of Adam and Eve,
but she gave birth to children. This raises a question
in my mind. Since there was a second woman
in the land of Nod, and she had children with Cain,
does this mean that some of us are only half sinners?

Letters to the Lord – XVII
Killing Love

Dear Lord,

I've been reading Your book,
trying to understand how humankind
arrived at the point it is today.
In the beginning, You created
Adam and Eve, they produced
two sons, and man killed man.

As time passed, You were unhappy
with humankind, so You sent a flood,
killing all but Noah and his family,
and man killed man. Moses rescued
the children from bondage in Egypt
and taught Joshua to rape, kill and plunder,
and man killed man.

Jesus came teaching, *Love your neighbor*
as yourself, and man killed man.
In an effort to spread its teaching,
the church took up the cross
by fighting wars, sending armies
on crusades, burning witches,
and man killed man.

Today, war between religions
continues around the world,
each one claiming to speak
in Your name, and man kills man.

Lord, was this all a part of Your original
design, or is it an experiment gone awry?

Letters to the Lord – XVIII

Family Feud

Dear Lord,

I write today because
the world I live in is full of hate,
and the seeds for much of it seem
to have been planted by Your words.

In Your book, You promise to make
a great nation from the two sons of Abraham:
Isaac born of Sarah and Ishmael born
of Hagar, the slave girl of Sarah.

History shows a religion evolving
from each of these sons, and they
have now been at war for thousands
of years, each claiming to speak for You.

Untold numbers have died and many
thousands more have been crippled
while these religions try to prove they
are fighting for Your cause.

Lord, is this what You intended when
You made Your promises? Is it still
necessary that all the world continue
to suffer because of this family feud?

Letters to the Lord – XIX
By Knife or Stones

Dear Lord,

TV evangelists inflame their believers
by preaching against a woman's right
to abort a fetus, giving no exception
for incest, rape or the woman's life.

In Your book, You indicate You
know us as soul before the body is
formed in the womb. If we as soul,
exist independent of the physical
body, does it harm soul if the fetus
is aborted before soul takes residence?

Your book says if we
have stubborn children, we should
take them to the city elders
to be stoned to death.

Keeping in mind that You have said
we should not add to or take away
from Your word, is it more acceptable
in Your sight to raise every fetus,
regardless of circumstance, until
stubbornness is detected, and then
stone the child to death?

Letters to the Lord – XX
Death Penalty

Dear Lord,

Many in our land would hang the Ten Commandments in our halls of justice, an attempt to give religious law power over civil law.

If this comes to pass, Lord, should we require our judges
to issue punishment as you have commanded in Your book?

Taking the Lord's name in vain: death. Working on the Sabbath, cursing father or mother, adultery and many more: death.

To implement this plan would take an army of executioners.
Adding adulterers would compound the numbers a thousandfold.

If executioners are forced to work seven days a week, would this make them candidates for their own execution?

Lord, how can I reconcile these commands with *Thou shall not kill?*

Letters to the Lord – XXI

Love-Hate

Dear Lord

We are taught Your book is without flaw,
every chapter sacred, every word true.

In Deuteronomy, *You* say if I have family,
friends, or know anyone near or far away
that believes in another God, I should
show them no pity, but kill them by
my own hand.

You continue: *What thing soever I command you,
observe to do it: thou shalt not add thereto,
nor diminish from it.*

Jesus taught that I should love
my enemies, turn the other cheek,
do good to those that despise me.

Lord, do you understand my confusion?
Which teaching is flawless and true?

Must I be like the terrorist, killing
all that do not believe as I do,
or should I turn the other cheek,
and find a way to love my enemies?

Lord, please answer soon because
they that believe in other gods
are everywhere, and I don't know
if I should kill or love them.

Letters to the Lord: Bible References, King James Version

Letter I	Numbers 31:14-18; Deuteronomy 21:18-21
Letter II	Genesis Chapters 7 and 8
Letter III	Genesis 1:28, 3:6-7
Letter IV	Jeremiah 1:5
Letter V	John 3:16; Genesis 6:2-4
Letter VI	Joshua 10:12-13
Letter VII	Jeremiah 1:5; Matthew 11:7-15, 17:10-13
Letter VIII	Revelation 7:1; 1 Corinthians 13:12
Letter IX	Isaiah 7:1-16, 8:3-4; 2 Chronicles 28:1-5; Deuteronomy 18:18-22
Letter X	Isaiah 7:14; Matthew 1:20-23; Luke 1:26-31; Matthew 2:13-14, 2:19-20
Letter XI	Genesis 1:27
Letter XII	Matthew 1:6-16, Luke 3:23-31
Letters XIII	Christian Bible and Church History
Letters XIV	Joshua 10:10-40
Letters XV	Mark 13:26-30; Matthew 16:27-28

Letters XVI	Genesis 4:16-17
Letter XVII	Bible and religious history
Letter XVIII	Genesis 17:19-20, 21:13
Letter XIX	Jeremiah 1:5; Deuteronomy 12:32, 21:18-21
Letter XX	Exodus 31:14-16, 35:2; Leviticus 20; Matthew 15:4
Letters XXI	Deuteronomy 12:32, 13:6-10; Matthew 5:43-44

Colophon

Titles set in Mona Lisa Solid
Text set in Minion Pro
Using Adobe Indesign
Digitally Printed inUSA

www.onespiritpress.com
onespiritpress@gmail.com

www.ingramcontent.com/pod-product-compliance
Lightning Source LLC
LaVergne TN
LVHW010101110826
845155LV00028B/431

* 9 7 8 1 8 9 3 0 7 5 7 8 8 *